BEST OF KYOTO
YOUR #1 ITINERARY PLANNER FOR WHAT TO SEE, DO, AND EAT

Wanderlust Pocket Guides

Best of Kyoto
Your #1 Itinerary Planner for What to See, Do, and Eat

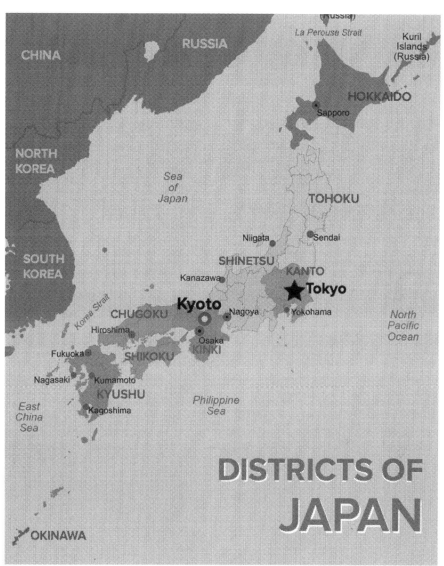
Map of Japan

Planning a trip to Japan?
Check out our other Wanderlust Pocket Travel
Guides:

BEST OF TOKYO: YOUR #1 ITINERARY PLANNER FOR
WHAT TO SEE, DO, AND EAT

BEST OF JAPAN: YOUR #1 ITINERARY PLANNER FOR
WHAT TO SEE, DO, AND EAT

Table of Contents

INTRODUCTION

Arashiyama, Kyoto

In this ancient Japanese *City of Ten Thousand Shrines*, culture, history, and natural beauty come together to compose pieces of stunning art that can only exist here, and nowhere else. Reputedly the most beautiful city in Japan, Kyoto contains 20% of Japan's national treasures, and 14% of its important cultural properties. There are also 17 UNESCO World Heritage Sites in the region.

Located in the center of the Island of Honshu, Kyoto has a population of about 1.5 million. Until 1868, it served as the capital of imperial Japan for more than one thousand years. Today, it is the 7th largest city, and a major part of the Kyoto-Osaka-Kobe metropolitan area, not to mention arguably Japan's most important cultural and historical site.

Kyoto is also one of the few Japanese cities to have escaped allied bombings during World War II. As a result, Kyoto has kept many of its pre-war buildings, such as the traditional townhouses known as *machiya*, no longer found elsewhere. While Kyoto has undergone continuous modernization, and replaced some older buildings with newer architecture, like the Kyoto Station complex, you still come to this city for a taste of its long, epic, and often intriguing story.

If you want to learn, Kyoto will offer to teach you nearly the entirety of Japan's long history. If you are receptive, Kyoto will show you one-of-a-kind landscapes you are not likely to ever forget.

HOW TO USE THIS GUIDE

In this pocket guide, we introduce to you the most interesting and unique allures Kyoto has to offer. The most ancient temples in Japan are found here, along with imperial palaces, and stunning natural vista. For our recommendation on the highlights of the city, look to Kyoto at a Glance, which links to detailed information on these sights and experiences in the guide. Check out the Planning section to see how you should prepare for your trip, and the Transportation section for how you can get around between all the fun things you will be doing in Kyoto.

Most of Kyoto's best sights are located in five areas – Central, West (Arashiyama), East (Higashiyama), North, and South. Within each area, we will discuss the best sights, experiences and also our recommendations for shopping, restaurants, hotels, and nightlife in those areas, so you can build meals and entertainments into your itinerary. In addition, we have easy to follow itineraries, including Day Trips to Uji and Himeji, and easy stopovers at nearby gems, Osaka and Nara.

Enjoy your trip - it is sure to be one of the most unforgettable experiences of your life!

SYMBOLS LEGEND

Sights and Attractions
(**) We indicate the absolutely must-see sights and attractions with two asterisks after their name.
(*) We indicate the highly recommended sights and attractions with one asterisk after their name.

Restaurants
Average meal cost:
$ - less than $10 (USD)
$$ - $11 USD - $ 25 (USD)
$$$ - $ 25 – 50 USD and up (USD)
$$$$ - $ 50 and up (USD)

Hotels
$ - less than $100 (USD)
$$ - $101- $150 (USD)
$$$ - $ 151 and up (USD)

KYOTO AT A GLANCE

Known as the "City of Ten Thousand Shrines", Kyoto has more UNESCO sites than you can imagine, or have the time to see all on one trip. In this guide, we introduce you to only the best, most unique and intriguing sights and experiences in this ancient city older than Japan itself.

Look across a tranquil pond at the shimmering roof of the **Kinkaku-ji**, known also as the "Golden Pagoda", the most splendid shrine complex in Kyoto. Ascend the wooden veranda of the **Kiyomizu-dera Temple**, elevated by hundreds of pillars, for incredible views of the whole city. Stroll down the scenic, cherry blossom-lined pedestrian path known as **Philosopher's Walk**, and hit a few of the amazing shrines along the way, each with a charm of its own. Had enough of tranquil gardens? Head to the playful **Fushimi Inari Shrine**, dedicated to Japan's fox goddess, and don't miss the street market full of special local food leading up to its gate. After taking in the garden and pond designed by Zen master Musō Soseki at **Tenryu-ji Temple**, walk through the sprawling, often photographed **Bamboo Forest** in Arashiyama. Be sure to visit the Japanese macaque monkeys at the famous **Iwatayama Monkey Park**, and buy some peanuts for these furry little guys. After seeing all ten thousand shrines, or any portion thereof, get a glimpse of the imperial center of ancient Japan in **Nijo Castle**, before relaxing on the beautifully curated grounds of the **Imperial Park**.

Seeing alone is not enough, you have to participate in Kyoto's ancient heritage. Hitch a ride with a **rickshaw**, now pulled exclusively by charming and attractive men, who also happen to be very knowledgeable about local history. Join in the **zen meditation** sessions at a temple, and find your center under the guidance of some of the wisest men in the world. Take a **riverboat cruise** down Hozu River, and experience the charming Arashiyama district to its fullest. Join a walking tour in the **Gion**

Geisha District, while perfectly made up real-life working geishas scurry past you to their next appointment. With some time to spare, take a short trip to nearby historical **Uji**, the tea capital of Japan, and experience the traditional **tea ceremony**.

With so many shrines and temples, Buddhist monks' simple fares have been elevated to an art form in Kyoto - try **Shigetsu** for an immersive and beautiful experience, or specialty tofu at **Yudofuya Restaurant**. After tea ceremonies, try something more down to earth at **Kasagiya**, which specializes in tea and local desserts. **Nishiki Market**, known as "Kyoto's Pantry" offers plenty of traditional snacks you can walk and eat. For a splurge, look no further than premium wagyu beef, at **Otsuka**.

BEST OF KYOTO

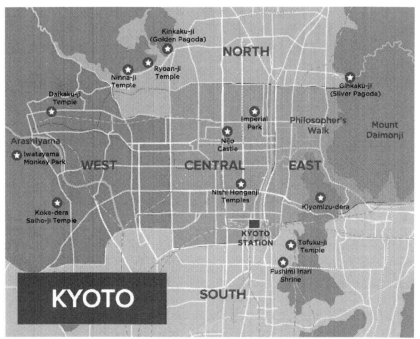

Map of Kyoto – Featuring Top Attractions

CENTRAL KYOTO

Here in Central Kyoto lies the urban center of the former imperial capital, in other words, the heart of the heart of this ancient culture. Toward the northern tip of the district are the carefully tended gardens, and stately buildings of the Imperial Palace. But as you stroll away from historical sites, you will come across the ultra-modern showpiece structure of Kyoto Station. Here then in Central Kyoto is the embodiment of the city today: a marbled mix of old and new, a place of thousands of years of history moving rapidly forward into the future.

See

Reference: Symbols legend (*/$/$$/$$$)

Nijo Castle**
Nijo Castle, the one-time power center of the imperial regime, is now one of the most noteworthy highlights of Kyoto. This complex, with its tastefully curated gardens and splendid centuries-old structures, was the official Kyoto residence of the "shogun", or the head of defense of imperial Japan, dating back to the 1600's.

The grounds consist of two concentric rings of fortifications, the Ninomaru Palace, the ruins of the Honmaru Palace, various support buildings and several gardens. Pay special attention to the series of ornately-decorated reception rooms within the Ninomaru Palace, with its famous "nightingale floor" - the intricate wooden flooring makes bird-like squeaking sounds when stepped on, to give advance warning when someone is approaching.

Rent an audio guide in English at the front entrance if you want to learn more about the rich history of the castle. Most signs are also in English.

Tip
Avoid the early morning hours, when tour groups flood the place. Late morning or lunch hour would be a much better choice. If possible, also avoid the summer, when Japanese school children are taken to these historical sites in hoards.

Address: 541 Nijojo-cho, Horikawa-nishiiru, Kyoto

Imperial Park**
This sprawling and peaceful complex in the center of Kyoto, contains the Kyoto Imperial Palace, the Sento Imperial Palace, and vast grounds home to 50,000 trees, including cherry, plum, and peach tree orchards.

Kyoto Imperial Palace is a reconstruction of the original, dating from 1855. Although the current imperial family does not actually spend much time here, it nonetheless provides interesting insight into the lives of the imperial court.

Sento Imperial Palace, or Sento Gosho, served as the residence of retired emperors during the Edo era. Today, Sento is essentially a private park within the larger palace complex. There is a guided tour, but you may wish to just hang out and soak in the peaceful green splendor of the place that will make you forget all about the bustles of the city outside.

Address: 3 Kyoto-Gyoen Kamigyo-ku, Kyoto 602-0881, Kyoto

Nishi Hongan-ji Temple*
The name "Nishi Hongan-ji" means "Western Temple of the Original Vow". This World Heritage Site dates back to the early 1600's, when the ruling shogun at the time split the leading main temple into two, the other being "Higashi Hongan-ji", the "Eastern Temple of the Original Vow", in order to diminish the power of the Jōdo Shinshu sect of Buddhism. Today, Nishi Hongan-ji is the head temple of the Jōdo sect. Entrance is free.
Address: Horikawa-dori hanayamachi-sagaru, Shimogyo-ku, Kyoto

Toji Temple*
The pagoda in Toji Temple has the honor of being the tallest such structure in Japan. But other buildings in this temple are just as impressive with surprisingly colorful interiors, and a variety of precious Buddhist sculptures on display. The rest of the temple grounds consists of a relaxing garden that is a great cherry blossom viewing spot in the spring. There is also a flea market, which is held on the 21st of every month.
Address: 1 Kujyomachi, Minami-ku, Kyoto

Higashi Hongan-ji

The majestic main hall of the Eastern Temple, is said to be the largest wooden structure in the world. It can accommodate up to 5,000 people, and serves as the headquarter of the Shinju sect. Check out Shosei-en Garden, which includes the Ingetsu Pond, designed to look like the Shiogama coast in Miyagi Prefecture. Entrance is free.
Address: 754 Tokiwacho, Karasumadori Shichijo-agaru,Kyoto

Kyoto Tower
Go up to the top of the Kyoto Tower to get a panoramic view of Kyoto's urban sprawl.
Address: Karasuma Shichijo sagaru, Shimogyo-ku,Kyoto

Kyoto Manga Museum*
The unassuming old elementary school building holds over 300,000 manga-related items, ranging from rare Meiji-era publications, to works of well-known contemporary artists you may be familiar with. You can pick out and read anything from the "Wall of Manga" - some 50,000 volumes arranged on shelves running along the building's corridors.
Address: Karasuma-dori Oike-agaru, Kyoto

Museum of Kyoto
This museum on the history of Tokyo features many ancient artifacts. If you are a history buff with an interest in ancient pottery, be sure to check it out.
Address: 623-1 Higashikatamachi, Nakagyo-ku, Kyoto

Umekoji Steam Locomotive Museum
This former locomotive depot features a 20-track roundhouse surrounding a turntable that houses and exhibits 19 preserved steam locomotives.
Address: Kankijicho, Shimogyo-ku, Kyoto

Do

Nishiki Market**

Literally named the "brocade market", Nishiki Market is known to locals as "Kyoto's Pantry", as it is easily the best traditional food market in the city. You'll find all the major ingredients of traditional Kyoto cuisine here: tsukemono (Japanese pickles), fresh tofu, Kyo-yasai (Kyoto's specialty vegetables), wagashi (Japanese sweets), tea, and fresh fish and shellfish. You can also eat as you go - sample from stalls peddling yakitori (meat cooked on skewers) and sashimi - or sit down at a restaurant found amid the shops. You might even score some exotic whale meat if you are lucky!

Location: Nishikikoji-dori, Nakagyo-ku (between Teramachi and Takakura)

Toji Flea Market*

On the 21st of each month, Toji Temple hosts a large flea market on its temple grounds, featuring long rows of vendors selling food and an eclectic assortment of odds and ends, from elegant Japanese crafts and rare plants, to piles of old postcards, photos, movie posters, and appliances from decades past.

Address: Toji Temple, 1 Kujyomachi, Minami-ku, Kyoto

Nishijin Textile Center

You can learn about the history of the famous Nishijin textiles, dress up as a geisha, or try your hand at weaving. Check out the Kimono Show - two floors displaying the process of silk making and the history of kimono.

Address: Horikawa Dori, Kyoto

Eat

Pontocho Area

Take a night stroll down this narrow lane running from Shijo-dori to Sanjo-dori, one block west of the Kamo River. Pontocho is one of the Kyoto's most traditional nightlife districts. You'll find anything from super-exclusive geisha houses to common yakitori bars.

Tip
Feel free to visit any establishment with a menu and listed prices. Avoid others to be safe.

Chao Chao Sanjo Kiyamachi
$
Japanese
Kick back with some pork or shrimp gyoza, pan-fried dumplings, and good drinks. For dessert, try the chocolate gyoza with ice cream.
Address: 117 Ishiyacho Kiya-Machi Sanjo Kudaru Nakagyo-Ku,Kyoto

Demachi Futaba
$
Japanese, Dessert
Try one, or several, of the great variety of red bean based Japanese dessert at this store.
Address: 236 Seiryucho, Kamigyo-ku, Kyoto 602-0822

Menbakaichidai
$$
Japanese, Noodles
Sit at the bar, and chat with the father and son team at Menbakaichidai as they prepare your bowl of ramen. Order the "fire ramen" for a little surprise show.
Address: 757-2 Minamiiseyacho Kamigyo-Ku, Kyoto 602-8153

Hafuu Honten
$$$
Japanese and French Fusion
Prepare for the best steak of your life! This Japanese and French fusion restaurant is a little out of the way in Kyoto's Central district, but is by all accounts, worth the short hike. The headliner

here at Hafuu Honten is premium wagyu beef - stewed, thinly-sliced, grilled, and every other way, all of them incredible. There are also plenty of good wine and delicious desserts to round out what many claim will be, the absolute best meal of your trip to Japan.
Address: 471-1 Sasayacho, Nakagyo-ku, Kyoto 604-0983

Yoshikawa Inn Tempura
$$$$
Japanese, Tempura
If you are going to splurge on one meal, make it here. Forget what tempura you've had at the Japanese restaurant back home, because they hardly deserve the name next to Yoshikawa's offerings. Sit at the bar and watch the chef work his magic on the freshest ingredients, perfectly fried.
Address: 135 Matsushitacho, Tominokojidori Oike-sagaru, Nakagyo-ku, Kyoto 604-8093

Nightlife

Fishbowl
Bar
Great, English-speaking bar, great care is put into the cocktails at Fishbowl.
Address: Kiyamachi Sanjo agaru Osaka-cho, Nakagyo-ku, Kyoto 604-8001

WESTERN KYOTO (ARASHIYAMA)

Arashiyama is tucked along the base of the Arashiyama Mountains (meaning "Storm Mountains"), about 30 minutes to the west of Central Kyoto. Still, it is well worth the trip for the number of great sights here. Walk quickly upriver through the main street of the district, along with the famous Togetsu-kyo Bridge, which forms the heart of Arashiyama and can be quite the tourist circus, and you will be rewarded with Kameyama-koen Park, Tenryu-ji Temple, and the stunning Bamboo Grove.

See

Tenryu-ji Temple**
Considered one of Kyoto's five Great Zen Temples, Tenryu-ji Temple is a UNESCO World Heritage Site and the main temple of the Rinzai sect of Buddhism in Kyoto. The original temple building dates back to the 14th century, but the current is a reconstruction from the last century. Do take a leisurely stroll around the lovely garden and pond, both designed by Zen master Musō Soseki. Afterwards, exit through the north gate, walk through the splendid bamboo forest to reach the Ōkōchi Sansō villa (see below).
Address: 68 Saga Tenryuji Susukinobabacho, Ukyo-ku, Kyoto

Arashiyama Bamboo Forest*
The beautiful bamboo forest is one of the most photographed sights in Kyoto, but no picture can do justice to the sense of wonder you feel standing in the midst of this sprawling bamboo grove. It is unlike any forests you may have seen before.

Okochi Sanso Villa*
This splendid mountain retreat used to belong to the Japanese silent film legend Ōkōchi Denjirō. The grounds are beautiful throughout the year, but are at their best in the fall, when trees explode into fiery shades of red and gold. Take a walk through the

villa's beautiful gardens while savoring the fine views of the city below, before dropping by the small museum dedicated to the former owner's life and work.
Address: 8-3 Sagaogurayama Tabuchiyamacho, Ukyo-ku, Kyoto

Iwatayama Monkey Park**
When you have gotten enough of temples and shrines in the city, take some time off to feed the macaque monkeys in this park. Don't bring food with you - the monkeys prefer the peanuts on sale inside the shack on top of the mountain inside the park. They also seem fond of the keeper's motorcycle, which is usually parked next to the shack.
Address: 8 Genrokuyamacho, Nishikyo-ku, Kyoto

Daikakuji Temple
Originally the villa of Emperor Saga, today Daikakuji is known as the birthplace of Saga Goryu, a school of the Japanese art of flower arrangement. You will often find stunning arrangements near the entrance to the temple, and the Osawanoke Pond inside is also very relaxing.
Address: 4 Saga, Osawa-cho, Kyoto 616-8411, Kyoto

Nonomiya Shrine
Women once underwent training at this small shrine inside the bamboo forest before becoming shrine maidens at Ise Shrine, the holiest Shinto shrine in Japan.
Address: 1 Saga Nonomiyacho, Ukyo-ku, Kyoto

Toei Studio Park
Explore this unique park featuring movie sets from famous Japanese TV shows.
Address: 10 Higashi-Hachigaokacho, Uzumasa, Ukyo-ku, Kyoto

Otagi Nenbutsu Temple*
You won't find it in many guidebooks, but Otagi Nenbutsu Temple is truly one of Kyoto's best hidden gems. Originally dating back to the 8th century, the temple has by turns been

destroyed by flood, fire, and typhoon. Two fierce statues guard the gate to this temple, which hosts 1,200 small statues, each with a unique and memorable character. The best part is, you can explore this explosion of "personalities" in relative seclusion.
Address: 2-5 Saga Toriimotofukatanicho, Ukyo-ku,Kyoto 616-8439

Kokedera**
Also known as Saiho-ji, Kokedera is a World Heritage Sites famous for its beautiful moss garden. Visit in summer or autumn, when the garden is at the height of its beauty.

Unlike other temples, Kokedera has a strict reservation process in order to limit the number of visitors, and avoid having too many people step on and kill the moss. At least one week prior to your visit, preferably at least three, you should send a letter giving your name, the number of people in your party, and the dates you prefer to visit along with a self-addressed stamped envelope, at Saiho-ji Temple, 56 Jingatani-cho, Matsuo Nishikyo-ku, Kyoto, 615-8286, Japan.

If you are in Japan already, request an "ofuku hagaki". If outside Japan, you can request an International Reply Coupon (IRC) to cover the postage. The temple will let you know whether you have been accepted, and what day and time you have been scheduled. You'll want to be flexible in your schedule as the temple may suggest a day earlier or later. Be very punctual, otherwise you will be denied entry.

Tip
If accepted, you will pay 3,000 yen upon admission. The ticket includes listening to a monk recite sutras, which is quite an experience, but does require you to sit on your legs or crosslegged for nearly an hour. Request a low chair if you think sitting on the floor will be a problem for you.

Address: 56 Matsuo Jingatanicho, Nishikyo-ku, Kyoto

Katsura Imperial Villa*
This cultural treasure is famous for its magnificent gardens and fine classical architecture. As with other imperial buildings in Kyoto, you must obtain permission to join a free tour through the Imperial Household Agency, either through their website or through the office near the Imperial Palace. Slots are extremely limited, so be sure to apply well in advance of your visit.
Address: Katsuramisono, Nishikyo-ku, Kyoto

Matsuo Taisha Shrine*
Dating to before the establishment of Kyoto as Japan's capital, this shrine is off the beaten path and popular for local sake brewers to come and pray. The water is famously pure, and the garden is notably beautiful.
Address: 3 Arashiyama-miyamachi, Kyoto

Suzumushi-dera Temple
Enjoy tea, a snack, and a speech by one of the temple's monks at Suzumushi-dera, which means "cricket temple", before listening to the large case of crickets chirping away. This place is great to visit in the winter, as they keep the temple quite warm for the crickets, allowing you to warm your chilly hands as well.
Address: 31 Matsumuroike, Nishikyo-ku, Kyoto

Do

Hozu River Cruise
Catch a boat ride down the Hozu River, so you can experience Arashiyama to the fullest. You will find boats waiting on either side of the river, but confirm how far and for how long the trip goes. Cruises range between 20 minutes to two hours. Be prepared to get splashed, and dress appropriately.
Address: 2 Shimonakajima Hozucho, Kameoka 621-0005, Kyoto

Sagano Romantic Train

The scenic ride on a steam train through Arashiyama. Trains depart from Torokko Saga Station every hour, and take you as far as Kameoka. Many people take the train, then take the Hozu River Cruise to get back to Arashiyama.
Address: Saga Tenruji, Ukyo-ku, Kyoto

Shopping along Tenryuji Tsukurimichi-cho
You will find many of the area's best shops and dining options along this stretch of land which runs from the Togetsu-kyo Bridge, up to Seiryo-ji Temple.

Eat

Hirokawa
$$
Japanese
You are here for eel, or in Japanese, unagi. At Hirokawa, that unagi comes perfectly grilled, lightly-coated in sauce, served over rice. Yum!
Address: Sagatenryujikitatsukurimichicho, Ukyoku, Kyoto 616-8374

Shoraian
$$$
Japanese
There is no better place to try the regional specialty, tofu, than at Shoraian. You will be served in a historic villa, sitting on tatamis, overlooking a river. Enjoy each course, perfectly portioned and expertly assembled into little dishes of art.
Address: Kanyuchinai, Sagakamenoocho, Ukyo-ku, Kyoto 616-8386

Shigetsu
$$$
Japanese, Vegetarian
Shigetsu will show you what "vegetarian" really means. Sitting on the ground of this temple garden, you will be served delicate

dishes that are the traditional fares of the monks in Kyoto, including tofu, which is a regional specialty.

Address: 68 Sagatenryujisusukinobabacho, Tenryuji Temple, Ukyo-ku, Kyoto 616-8385

Otsuka
$$$
Japanese, Steakhouse
Great place to sample wagyu beef. Like other steakhouses serving this premium cut, Otsuka is a little expensive, running between 3,500 yen to 6,000 yen for a set meal. But you know that your food will arrive perfectly cooked.

Address: 20-10 Sagatenryuji Setogawacho, Ukyo-ku, Kyoto 616-8376

Hiranoya
$$$$
Japanese
Enjoy the quiet ambience at this teahouse and restaurant, along with its perfectly-prepared food.

Address: Sagatoriimotosennocho, Ukyo-ku, Kyoto 616-8437

EASTERN KYOTO (HIGASHIYAMA)

Arguably the most important tourist district in Kyoto, the eastern region of the city - Higashiyama - could easily take a full day of sightseeing. Consider starting from Kiyomizu-dera, and walk north through Gion, and visit Yasaka Shrine and Nanzen-ji, before following the Philosopher's Walk to Ginkaku-ji.

See

Kyomizu-dera Temple**
Incredible views of the city from the temple complex's elevated main hall, which has a wooden veranda supported by hundreds of pillars, is Kyomizu-dera's major attraction. But you can also stop by the love-themed Jishu Shrine, and purchase a charm to help win the affections of the one you love, or walk with your eyes closed between the "love stones" positioned 18 meters apart, to confirm your loved one's affection. There is also the waterfall, under which you can stand and collect water to drink with a little tin cup. Lastly, if you are up for a workout, take the path that leads into the mountain and take in the lovely forest and green scenery.
Address: 1-294 Kiyomizu, Higashiyama-ku, Kyoto

Sanjusangen-do**
From the street, this walled compound does not look like much. But once inside this ancient temple dating back to 1164, you will find a peaceful and spiritual place, with 1001 beautiful wooden and gold-leaf covered statues of Kannon, the Buddhist goddess of mercy, housed in 33 bays in the main hall. Afterwards, stroll in the garden and splash your face with refreshing spring water, and take a minute to meditate in the tranquility.
Address: 657 Sanjusangendo Mawaricho, Kyoto

Mt. Daimonji

The best view of the city is just an hour's hike, through a pleasant forest walk, up Mt. Daimonji. At the summit, take a break and take in your surroundings. The overachievers can continue to hike through the forest for hours, but beware that you may end up far away from where you started.

Kyoto National Museum
In this museum near Sanjusangen-do, you'll find a huge collection of ancient Japanese sculpture, ceramics, metalwork, painting, and other historical artifacts. Confusingly, there is a statue of Rodin's The Thinker out front, the museum's only western piece.
Address: 527 Chayamachi, Higashiyama-ku, Kyoto

Heian Shrine
Built as a scaled-down replica of the original Imperial Palace in 1895, Heian Shrine is now a popular place for cherry blossom viewing in the spring, and one of the most beautiful gardens in the city.
Address: 97 Okazaki Nishitennocho, Sakyo-ku, Kyoto

Sakura Season

Maruyama Park

Of all the amazing cherry blossom viewing opportunities in Kyoto, Maruyama Park boasts of the acknowledged best. The main attraction of the park is a weeping cherry tree. Note that it can get very crowded in the spring.

Address: 473 Maruyamacho, Higashiyama-ku, Kyoto

Kodaiji Temple*

This temple was built by Tokugawa Ieyasu, a renowned Japanese warlord, for the widow of his predecessor, Toyotomi Hideyoshi. Aside from the temple building and a nice garden, there is a bamboo grove that you can walk through on your way out.

Address: 526 Kodaiji Shimo-Kawaramachi, Higashiyama-ku, Kyoto

Chion-in Temple*

Beyond the largest Sanmon gate in the nation, you will find the magnificent head temple of the Jodo sect of Buddhism here. You can walk freely around the complex and see the buildings for free, but will have to pay a fee to see the "Seven Wonders" of the temple.

Address: 400 Hayashi-shita-cho 3-chome, Kyoto

Shoren-in Temple

During the Tokugawa period, Shoren-in served as temporary lodging for a retired emperor after the Imperial Palace burned down. Today, Shoren-in is considered one of the top five Tendai sect Buddhist temples in Japan. In November, you may get the chance to practice a tea ceremony. See "Do" section for more details.

Address: 69-1 Awataguchi Sanjobocho, Higashiyama-ku, Kyoto

Gion Geisha District **

Walk the flagstone-paved streets between traditional buildings of the Gion district, and watch real-life geishas hurry past you. Here in Gion District, the geisha culture is very much alive. The area just north of Shijo-dori, to the west of Yasaka Shrine, is especially photogenic,, especially around the two streets called Shinbashi-dori and Hanami-koji. The two sloping streets, Sannen-zaka and Ninen-zaka, are also great for pictures. Around 6pm or 9pm are good times to spot a geisha, as they will be leaving their boarding houses then. But please remember to be respectful - you don't want to be the obnoxious tourist chasing a poor girl for a picture, as they walk away as fast as possible.

Geishas

Yasaka Shrine
At the edge of Gion District, you will find the shrine responsible for Kyoto's main festival, the Gion Matsuri, which takes place in

July. Admission is free to the small shrine, which has an impressive display of lanterns.
Address: 625 Gion Kitagawa, Higashiyama-ku, Kyoto

Kennin-ji Temple
With its handsome halls, and sand and moss gardens, Kennin-ji is the oldest Zen temple in Japan. Art lovers will find the place particularly interesting, with its famed Edo-era screens of the Wind and Thunder Gods by Sotatsu, and Koizumi Junsaku's splendid Twin Dragons on the high ceiling of the Hatto Dharma Hall.
Address: 584 Yamatooji Yojo-sagaru Komatsucho, Higashiyama-ku, Kyoto

Philosopher's Walk**
This scenic pedestrian path follows a cherry-tree-lined canal between Ginkaku-ji and Nanzen-ji. The route is named after the influential 20th century Japanese philosopher and Kyoto University professor Nishida Kitaro, who is thought to have strolled the path daily for meditation. Along the way, you will find a number of Kyoto's best temples, including Hōnen-in, Ōtoyo Shrine, and Eikan-dō Zenrin-ji. The beautiful walk will take about 30 minutes, but most people spend more time visiting the sights along the way (listed below starting with Ginkaku-ji). During the cherry blossom season, or the fall when the leaves are changing color, you'll be hard pressed to find a prettier (or a more crowded, probably) walk anywhere else.

Ginkaku-ji**
Situated at the northern end of the Philosopher's Walk, Ginkaku, also known as the Silver Pavilion, is a popular spot with tourists that can get very crowded. The temple was built in 1482 by Shogun Ashikaga Yoshimasa, who modeled this retirement villa after his grandfather's retirement villa - Kinkaku-ji, the Golden Pavilion at the base of the northern mountains.

Most stroll through the dry Zen garden and the surrounding moss garden (a must-see!), before posing for pictures in front of the pavilion across a pond.
Address: 2 Ginkakuji-cho Sakyo-ku, Kyoto

Honen-in Temple
This quiet temple was built in honor of Honen, the founder of the Jodo sect. Take a look at the interesting raised sand designs in the garden.
Address: 30 Shishigatani Goshonodancho, Sakyo-ku, Kyoto

Eikan-do Zenrin-ji Temple**
Eikan-do, a Jodo sect Buddhist temple, is famous for its autumn foliage and the evening illuminations that take place in the fall. The main buildings are built along the base of the hillside, and are connected by wooden corridors you can walk through. The most recognized building of the complex is its Tahoto Pagoda, which is nestled in the trees on the hillside, overlooking the temple's other buildings. Notice that the first story of the pagoda is square, whereas the second is round. The view from the top of the pagoda is beautiful.

During the fall, the Hojo Pond in the temple's garden is also very attractive. Small streams run through the entire temple grounds and meet in this pond. There is a small shrine on an island in the middle of the pond.
Address: 48 Eikando-cho, Sakyo-ku, Kyoto

Nanzen-ji Temple**
You won't miss Nanzen-ji - it is the largest temple on Philosopher's Walk, and features a distinctive two-story entrance gate, along with an unusual Meiji-era aqueduct that would look right at home in Italy. Aside from the main temple, you can also take a look at the abbot's quarters, with its intimate garden and some impressive paintings on the sliding doors of the buildings. It is ¥300 to get in the gate, and another ¥300 to see the temple, and the moss garden dating back to the 13th century.

Address: 86 Nanzenji Fukuchicho, Sakyo-ku, Kyoto

Do

Philosopher's Path Walk
See above in "See" section.

Rickshaw Ride
Forget what you've seen in Hollywood films of poor, destitute rickshaw pullers. Kyoto's modern day rickshaw pullers are more than a cheap transport option, they are also knowledgeable tour guides eager to show you another side of the city. The men pulling today are highly regarded for keeping this cultural element alive, and often highly attractive. Some of the most popular pullers even have regular patrons.

You can find rickshaw drivers throughout the area from outside Maruyama Park to Kiyomizu-dera. They are particularly popular with couples, as it is quite a romantic experience, something like a horse carriage ride through Central Park. In general, pullers will have set routes, but you can also request to be taken to a specific attraction. Prices vary depending on which route you choose.

Geisha Walking Tour and Lecture
If you wanted to learn more about the exotic world of the Geisha, be sure to book a walking lecture, which includes entrance into a teahouse, a history lesson of the unique geisha culture, and numerous photo opportunities along the walk in the Gion district. You can book here: http://www.kyotosightsandnights.com/walking.html, for ¥3,000 per person.

Rakushisha Paper Crafts Shopping
This great little souvenir shop has some of the more original and less tacky souvenirs you'll find in Kyoto. Try replicas of famous

Japanese paintings that are much less cheesy than those you'll find along Shijo or near Kiyomizu-dera, or authentic Kyoto-made paper fans that would be hard to find elsewhere.
Address: 549-2 Nishinomoncho, Higashiyama-ku, Kyoto

Eat

Kasagiya
$
Tea
Between temples, drop by this little traditional tea shop for a cup of Japanese matcha and snack on sweet glutinous riceballs.
Address: 349 Masuyacho Higashiyamaku, Kyoto 605-0826

Arabica Kyoto
$
Coffee
Amazing cup of coffee situated between the temples.
Address: 87-5 Hoshinocho, Higashiyama-ku, Kyoto 605-0853

Senmonten
$
Chinese
Great place to relax, grab a beer, and some incredible pan-fried dumplings.
Address: Higashiyama-ku | Higashi-gawa, Hanamikoji Shimbashi kudaru, Kyoto 605-0084

Karako
$$
Japanese, Noodles
Karako specializes in cheap and comforting food, specifically, ramen noodles and fried chicken.
Address: 12-3 Okazaki Tokuseicho, Sakyo-ku, Kyoto 606-8351

Omen
$$
Japanese, Noodles
A well-known udon noodle spot, reasonably-priced, quaint, delicious.
Address: Bus Pool South Ginkakuji Sakyoku, Kyoto 606-8406

Okariba
$$$
Japanese
Try out the most tender boar, trout, and other grilled delicacies while the owner of Okariba regales you with his wild hunting stories.
Address: 43-3 Okazaki Higashitenno-cho, Sakyo-ku | Residence Okazaki 1F, Kyoto

Hyotei
$$$$
Japanese
It's hard to say which is more beautiful - the food at Hyotei, or the vista. This three Michelin star restaurant serves its exquisite small dishes, "kaiseki" style, in individual rooms situated in a stunning ancient garden.
Address: Nanzenjikusagawacho, Sakyoku, Kyoto 606-8437

Nightlife

Pig & Whistle
Bar
Pig & Whistle is an expat favorite. Staff and patrons of this bar come from all over the world. You can play pub favorite games like billiard and darts while enjoying your beer.
Address: Shobi building 2F, 115 Ohashicho, Higashiyama-ku,Kyoto 605-0009

Jumbo Karaoke Hiroba

Karaoke
After some drinks at Pig & Whistle, drift to this karaoke joint is in the same building. There is a good selection of English songs, and the hourly rate includes the price of all drinks.
Address: Shobi building 2F, 115 Ohashicho, Higashiyama-ku,Kyoto 605-0009

Gael Irish Pub
Bar
A great pub and friendly escape for the travel-weary westerner.
Address: 236 Nijuikkencho, Higashiyama-ku, Kyoto 605-0077

Kick Up
Bar
Kick Up attracts a good mix of expats, locals and short-term travelers.
Address: Higashikomonoza-chō 331, Higashiyama-ku, Kyoto

Metro
Concert Hall
A great live music venue that hosts different themes every night. Dance in the disco section with Kyoto's most eclectic crowd.
Address: BF Ebisu Bldg, Kawabata-dōri, Marutamachi-sagaru, Sakyō-ku

Atlantis
Bar
This beautiful, trendy bar is one of the places expats congregate along with Kyoto's classiest crowd.
Address: 161 Matsumoto-chō, Ponto-chō-Shijō-agaru, Nakagyō-ku

A-Bar
Bar
Everything at this little izakaya is cheap. Really cheap - and that's why it's so popular with students. Look for the log cabin-looking building.

Address: 2nd fl, Reiho Kaikan, 366 Kamiya-chō, Nishikiyamachi-dōri, Shijō-agaru, Nakagyō-ku

NORTH KYOTO

This area of the city is home to many World Heritage Sites, including one of the city's most famous attractions - the magnificent golden pavilion of Kinkaku-ji Temple. Also look for the giant "大" symbol, meaning "big", burned on Mt. Daimon-ji, which can be climbed in an hour.

See

Kinkaku-ji Temple

Kinkaku-ji Temple**
Also known as the Temple of the Golden Pavilion, Kinkaku-ji is the most popular tourist attraction in Kyoto. It was originally built in the late 14th century as a retirement villa for Shogun Ashikaga Yoshimitsu, and later converted into a temple. The beautiful vista and the reflection of the luminous temple on the water makes for a striking photo - if you can keep the mobs of tourists out of it. Visit early to avoid the tour groups.
Address: 1 Kinkakuji-cho, Kita-ku, Kyoto

Ryoan-ji Temple**
This temple, styled in the "dry-landscape" style and famous for its Zen garden featuring an austere arrangement of 15 rocks on a bed of white gravel. The temple itself mirrors the simplicity of the garden, behind which is a stone washbasin called Tsukubai, said to have been contributed by Tokugawa Mitsukuni, a powerful feudal lord of the 17th century.
Address: 13 Ryoanji Goryonoshitacho, Kyoto

Ninna-ji Temple**
This large temple complex is often overlooked by tourists, so you can take your time to wander through its grounds and its beautiful walled garden. On the hills behind the temple, there is a miniature version of the renowned 88 Temple Pilgrimage in Shikoku - you can finish this one in an hour or two, rather than a month of two.
Address: 33 Omuro Ouchi, Kyoto 616-8092, Kyoto

Daitoku-ji Temple
There are many smaller temples within this large complex. Visit at the start of the day, and you may just have this tranquil place to yourself. Eight of the 24 sub-temples are open to the public for around ¥400 each. The most popular is Daisen-in, which features a beautiful Zen garden and a cinnamon sweet that only the temple has the right to produce and sell. Koto-in has beautiful maple trees.
Address: 53 Murasakino Daitoku-ji-cho, Kita-ku, Kyoto

Kitano Tenmangu Shrine
Michizane Sugawara was a prominent member of the Heian Court until he was exiled after falling out of favor with the emperor. The courtier died in exile, after which a series of natural disasters began to plague Kyoto. This shrine was built to appease Michizane's soul, and deified him as the God of Learning. Plum blossoms are beautiful here in early spring.
Address: 931 Bakuro-cho, Kyoto

Shimogamo Shrine*

Shimogamo Shrine, along with Kamigamo Shrine (below), are collectively known as the Kamo Shrines and have been highly revered by the Imperial Court since they were built in the earliest days of the city of Kyoto. Shimogamo is a great place to experience Japanese festivals, including the Aoi Matsuri, one of the top three festivals in the city. Legends have it that the forest surrounding the shrine, known as Tadasu no Mori, will reveal the secrets of those who enter. Do you dare?

Address: 59 Shimogamo Izumigawa-cho, Sakyo-ku, Kyoto

Kamigamo Shrine

One half of the Kamo Shrines, Kamigamo is known for the tatesuna, two large sand cones. Their original meaning is lost to history, but it has been speculated that they represent nearby mountains. Entrance is free.

Address: 339 Kamigamomotoyama, Kita-ku, Kyoto

Kyoto Botanical Garden

This large botanical garden, Japan's first, is popular with the Japanese for plum blossom viewing in February and early March, and cherry blossom viewing in April. There is also an indoor garden (with a nominal additional fee) featuring a wide range of plants, from tropical to desert.

Address: Shimogamohangicho, Sakyo-ku, Kyoto

Shugakuin Imperial Villa

Shugakuin, originally commissioned by Emperor Gomizuno-o in 1655, is separated into three villas. In the lower where the emperor relaxed before traveling upward, you'll see a garden with a tranquil stream running through it. The middle villa belonged to Princess Akinomiya, and contains beautiful art work, and a unique flat pine tree. Finally, upon entering the upper villa, you ascend the stairs for a breathtaking view of the garden and Yokuryu Pond. Cool fact: Princess Diana once visited Shugakuin!

Like other imperial properties in Kyoto, you will want to make a reservation ahead of time - 3 months if you can, for the best chances. Admission is free.
Address: 1-3 Shugakuin-yabusoe, Sakyo-ku, Kyoto

Shisendo Temple
Unlike other temples in the area, Shisendo is dedicated to the art of poetry. Originally built in 1641, it once housed famous poet Jozen Ishikawa, and now features portraits of 36 influential poets from ancient China. There is also a garden filled with azaleas.
Address: 27 Ichijoji Monguchi-cho, Sakyo-ku, Kyoto

Do

Zen meditation
There is no better place to try Zen meditation than in the ancient temples of Kyoto.

Shuko-in
The vice abbot at Shuko-in, Taka Kawakami, is American-educated. He leads a detailed English tour of the temple, and its Zen meditation lessons. The temple also hosts many important artistic and cultural properties related to Zen, with connections to Shinto and Christianity. Find more information here: http://www.shunkoin.com/.
Address: 42 Myoshiji-cho, Hanazono, Ukyo-ku, Kyoto

Taizo-in
Aside from a one-hour long meditation session, visitors are also treated to a brief tea ceremony, calligraphy lessons, and an English tour of the temple's garden. While you will need to make reservations at their website (http://www.taizoin.com/en/), and dedicate half a day to the session, the experience is a once-in-a-lifetime opportunity. Participants must be at least 15 years of age, so don't take the kids!

Address: Address: 35 Hanazono Myoshinjicho, Ukyo-ku, Kyoto

Kitano Tenmangu Flea Market
On the 25th of each month, Kitano hosts a flea market with vendors lined up along both sides of the pathway leading up to the complex, then extends around each side. You can find truly unique souvenirs for great prices, like pottery, porcelain, traditional dolls, clothing, and of course, delicious food.

Eat

Yudofuya Restaurant
Situated within the Ryoan-ji Temple is this delightful little tofu restaurant. You sit in a quiet room on tatami mats, and savor the special tofu hot pot and vegetarian lunch, while looking out to the exquisite garden with a tranquil pond. Speak in whispers only, to avoid disturbing the ambience.
Address: 13 Ryoanji Goryonoshitacho, Kyoto

Kurazushi
$
Sushi
Kurazushi serves "conveyor belt" sushi. At 100 yen a plate, each holding 2 pieces of sushi, this place is a steal. That doesn't mean the sushi is not fresh though, because as soon as each plate is placed on the conveyor, a hungry patron snatches it right up.
Address: 4 Hirano Miyajikicho Kita-ku, Kyoto 603-8365

SOUTH KYOTO

This part of the city stretches from the Oharano area in the west to Fushimi-ku, Daigo, and the southern tip of Higashiyama in the east. Some of the district's best attractions include Daigo-ji Temple, which is a World Heritage Site, and the endless lines of torii gates climbing up the mountainside, above Fushimi-Inari Shrine.

See

Fushimi Inari Shrine

<u>Fushimi Inari Shrine</u>**

Very often overlooked in the midst of Kyoto's countless temples, this jewel of a shrine is dedicated to Inari, Japan's fox goddess, and the head shrine for 40,000 Inari shrines across Japan. Walk up the hillside through the bright red torii gates, and take in the city from this elevated vantage point. Admission is free.

Address: 68 Fukakusa Yabunouchicho, Fushimi-ku, Kyoto

Daigo-Ji Temple*
Daigo-ji is old even by Kyoto standards. The oldest remaining structure in the temple is a five-story pagoda built in 951. The Sanboin Garden is truly beautiful, especially in autumn when leaves turn into vibrant bursts of color. Sadly, pictures are not allowed in the garden. The museum inside the temple is also worth checking out for the treasures it holds.
Address: 22 Daigo Higashi Oji-cho, Fushimi-ku, Kyoto

Fushimi Momoyama Castle
This castle was once a favorite of Toyotomi Hideyoshi, a preeminent daimyo, warrior, general, samurai, and politician in the 16th century, who is regarded as Japan's second "great unifier". The original structure was dismantled in 1623, but the current reconstruction contains a small museum and a gold-lined tea room.
Address: 45 Momoyamacho-Okura, Fushimi-ku, Kyoto

Tofuku-ji Temple
This large temple complex, with its many small and beautiful gardens, is popular with the Japanese for foliage during the fall months.
Address: 15-778 Hommachi, Higashiyama-ku, Kyoto

Oharano
Visit the Oharano area, to see a different side of Kyoto, and of Japan. The area has remained rural despite Japan's rapid modernization, and offers a charm of a bygone era all of its own. Most tourists do not know about it, so it is a nice change of pace for those wary of the crowds.

Oharano Shrine*
Imperial families have been making annual offerings at this shrine since xxx. Being quite removed from the city, this shrine offers a

peaceful surrounding that can be hard to find in Kyoto. It is not unusual to have the entire place to yourself. Admission is free.
Address: 1152 Oharano Minami Kasugacho, Nishigyo-ku, Kyoto

Shobo-ji Temple*
Opposite Oharano Shrine is this Shingon sect Buddhist temple featuring an impressive statue of the 3-faced thousand armed Kannon, and a beautiful Zen rock garden. You'll notice many of the rocks resemble animals, like a rabbit, or a frog.
Address: 1102 Kasuga, Minami, Oharano, SaIkyo-Ku, Kyoto

Shoji-ji Temple
Shoji-ji Temple is a great place to see cherry blossoms in the spring.
Address: 1194 Oharano Minamikasugacho, Nishikyo-ku, Kyoto

Eat

Around Fushimi Inari Shrine
Approaching the fox goddess shrine, you will find local delicacies sold roadside. Barbecued sparrow, or suzume, and sweetened sushi rice wrapped in fried tofu, or Inarizushi, are said to be the goddess' favorite food. Be sure to try them! Note that the sparrow is served on a skewer, still in its bird form, if you are squeamish about things like that.
Address: 68 Fukakusa Yabunouchicho, Fushimi-ku, Kyoto

DAY TRIPS FROM KYOTO

Uji

Take a quick detour to Uji from Kyoto, and see historical Japan as it has been for thousands of years, almost entirely unencumbered the developments of modernity. With a history as long as as that of its more famous neighbor, the ancient city of Uji has retained even more of its old-world charms than Kyoto. It is the scene of many famous Japanese stories, including the final chapters of the Tale of Genji, Japan's first novel. There are stores in this city that have been open for hundreds of years, and several important temples less trodden by Kyoto's hoards of tourists. Uji is also the tea capital of Japan, so be sure to partake in the many activities surrounding this culture.

Getting There

Uji is on the JR Nara Line. From Kyoto Station, it is just 17 minutes away via rapid train, or 27 minutes via local. The ticket costs ¥230.

You will arrive at the JR Uji station. There is a small tourist information center just outside, where you can grab a English map. Most sights are around here too, so just walk along the river while you are in Uji, and you will hit all the important spots!

See

Byōdō-in Temple
Byōdō-in was built in 1053, by Fujiwara Yorimichi, a chief advisor to the emperor. Originally a villa constructed by his father, Fujiwara converted Byōdō-in into a temple in anticipation of the coming of a dark age where Buddhism would disappear. Since its establishment, this temple became a refuge for the

faithful during many stretches of history, and gave rise to the Pure Land Faith movement of Buddhism.

You can walk around the grounds, and check out the museum that holds many of the temple's ancient artifacts. Unfortunately, the Phoenix Hall, the main structure of the temple - a picture of which is on the ¥10 coin - is under construction for 2015, so you won't be able to take the tour normally offered there.
Address: Renge-116, Uji, 611-0021

Ujigami Shrine
This modest little shrine is a World Heritage Site, and said to be the oldest Shinto shrine in Japan.
Address: 59 Uji Yamada, Uji 611-0021

Mimurotoji Temple
A great temple to visit for those who love flowers. There are flowers all over the mountainside and throughout the path in the garden, as well as beautiful lotus flowers planted in pots.
Address: 21 Todo Shigatani, Uji 611-0013

Taiho-an Tea House
There is no better place to experience a traditional Japanese tea ceremony than here in the tea capital of Japan. Taiho-an is operated by the government, this tea house right next to *Byōdō-in Temple* has both smaller, authentic tea rooms, and a larger room with a more relaxed atmosphere.
Address: 1-5 Uji, Togawa, Uji

HIMEJI

Located on the western edge of the Kansai region, Himeji is home to Japan's finest castle, the Himeji Castle. This splendid complex has been featured in many films about Japan, including The Last Samurai featuring Tom Cruise.

Getting There

The Hikari train, free of charge to Japan Rail Pass holders, gets you from Kyoto to Himeji in under an hour.

Once there, the castle and other important sights are only a ten to fifteen minute walk from the train station down Otemae-dōri street. Alternatively, you can take the sightseeing loop bus which only costs ¥100, and gets you to the castle in five minutes.

See

Himeji Castle
Also known as the "White Egret Castle", this shimmery white edifice on towering over the city of Himeji was built in the 1300's, and was once the biggest castle in all of Asia. Considered one of the most beautiful castles in Japan, it has luckily eluded the ravages of civil war, natural disasters, and the bombings of World War II.

Himeji Castle

Admission to Himeji is ¥1,000 adults and ¥300 children. A special combination ticket gets you into both the castle and the nearby Kōkoen Garden. There is a free guided tour in English, but only if a guide is available. Please note that since the castle reopened in March 2015 after several years of renovation, the number of visitors have soared. Go early, and expect to spend a few hours waiting in line. Avoid holidays and weekends if possible!
Address: 68 Hommachi, Himeji 670-0012

Kokoen Garden
Located next to Himeji Castle's outer moat, this magnificent collection of nine Edo-style walled gardens were laid out in 1992 on the site of ancient samurai houses. The gated partitions are faithful to the ruins of residential quarters, but within each enclosure, landscaped gardens and water features have been

established in place of the noble houses. There is also a tea arbor and a restaurant.
Address: 68 Honmachi, Himeji 670-0012

<u>Engyo-ji Temple</u>
You'll have to take the orange bus No. 8 from Himeji Castle for 30 minutes to reach Engyo-ji Temple, located in Mt. Shosha, but fans of Tom Cruise's *The Last Samurai* will not want to miss this beautiful temple, which served as the setting for the film. It is particularly in the fall, when the Japanese maples change color.
Address: 2968 Shosha, Himeji 671-2201

NARA

Dating back to the 700's, Nara is a capital more ancient than Kyoto. It would be a mistake to skip Nara in lieu of the more popular Kyoto, as it boasts of a collection of cultural and historical sights older than Kyoto's, just as preserved, and most importantly, far less crowded.

Getting There

From Kyoto Station, both the JR Nara Line and the private Kintetsu Kyoto Line will get you to Nara in about 35 minutes. There are several slower but cheaper train options as well.

After getting in, your best option to get around Nara is by bicycle. You can rent one just outside the JR station, for ¥700 a day. It is only 1km ride to Nara Park, where most major attractions are located.

See

<u>Nara Park</u>

This sprawling green space contains almost everything you'll want to see in Nara. The legend is that the god of Kasuga Taisha came to Nara riding a white deer, which enjoys protected status as envoys of the god. These cute little animals have gotten used to attention, and now just harass indulgent tourists and annoyed shopkeepers for biscuits.

Nara Deer Park, Nara

Tōdai-ji Temple
Home to Daibutsu, the largest Buddha statue in Japan, Tōdai-ji is a World Heritage Site, and includes the Daibutsu-den, which is said to be the largest wooden building in the world.
Address: 406-1 Zoshicho, Nara 630-8211

Kōfuku-ji
This Temple contains a three-story and a five-story pagoda, which contends with Toji pagoda for the title of the tallest pagoda in Japan.
Address: 48 Noborioji-cho, Nara

Nara National Museum

The national museum contains one of the world's best collections of Buddhist art, including an impressive collection of statues.
Address: 50 Noborioji-cho, Nara

Kasuga-yama Hill Primeval Forest
Enjoy a walk through this wild, undeveloped forest. The path is clearly marked.

Osaka

Osaka is, and has been many things. Dating back to the Asuka period in 500AD, it is one of Japan's oldest cities and its one-time capital. Even after the imperial capital moved elsewhere, Osaka continued to serve as a hub for land, sea, and river-canal transportation and commerce. In the Tokugawa era, the city emerged as the "Nation's Kitchen", the collection and distribution point for rice. During the Meiji era, Osaka's entrepreneurs led the country in industrial development. Bombing during World War II nearly obliterated this long historical heritage. After which, the city underwent a thorough, rapid, and by Japan's exacting standards, inelegant modern day reconstruction.

Today, Osaka is the third largest city in the country with a population of 3 million, and is known for its gruff appearance - even the ancient castle is a concrete reconstruction - and its open, brash, and above all, very funny inhabitants. Osaka is also acknowledged as Japan's best place to eat, drink, and party, beating out even Tokyo. Consider visiting Osaka before or after Kyoto - after days of temple hopping, Zen meditating, and nature gazing, you're sure to love all the modern fun Osaka has to offer!

Osaka

Getting There

You can fly directly into Osaka's airports, which also serves passengers wishing to visit Kyoto. Alternatively, several trains, both express and local, serve the Osaka-Kyoto line. See Transportation for more details.

Once you arrive, stick to the subway system, which is the second only to Tokyo in its extensive reach. The Midosuji Line will get you to most places you need to go - like train stations, and the shopping complexes of Shin-Osaka, Umeda, Shinsaibashi, Namba, and Tennoji. Signs and announcements are made in English as well as Japanese. Just one tip - keep the ticket stub! You'll need it to exit.

See

Osaka Castle
While this post-WWII reconstruction of the original Osaka Castle pales in comparison with other magnificent castles Japan has to offer, like Himeji Castle, it is still a popular destination for its huge collection of historical artifacts of the Osaka area. In the

spring, Osakans also love going to the castle's vast park for cherry blossom viewing and a picnic.
Address: 1-1 Osakajo, Chuo-ku, Osaka

Osaka Kaiyukan Aquarium
One of the largest public aquariums in the world and Osaka's most popular destination, Osaka Kaiyukan attracts huge crowds with its walk-through displays of marine life. Those traveling with children won't want to miss this! After spending a few hours learning about the sea, enjoy a ride on the 112.5 meter high Tempozan Ferris Wheel, for a panoramic view of the whole city.
Address: 1-1-10 Kaigan-dori, Minato-ku, Osaka

Umeda Sky Building
Built in the late 1980s, the Umeda Sky Building was originally envisioned as a "City of Air" in the form of four huge, interconnected towers. In the end, the city ended up with a 40-story, 173-meter building that, being so strangely shaped, has become one of Osaka's most recognizable landmarks. While offices occupy most of the 40 stories, there are markets and restaurants underground, and a rooftop observatory with an impressive view. The observatory is popular with Osaka's lovers - you can sit in a special seat with your loved one, each press a metal button to light up the ground around you into a heart. YOu can also purchase an engraved heart love for the padlock wall around the seat.
Address: 1-1-88 Oyodonaka, Kita-ku, Osaka 531-0076

Sumiyoshi Taisha Shrine
This Shinto shrine, one of Japan's oldest dating back to the 3rd century, is dedicated to three gods that protect the nation, sea voyages, and for promoting waka (31-syllable) poetry. The beautiful Sorihashi Bridge leads to the entrance of the main shrine grounds, and creats a uniquely high arch over a pond of black turtles.
Address: 2-9-89 Sumiyoshi, Sumiyoshi-ku, Osaka

Shitenno-ji Temple
This large, tranquil temple provides a bit of serenity in the bustling and loud city of Osaka. Originally built in 593 AD, what you see currently is a post-WWII reconstruction. Walk around the main hall and the garden, and if you'd like, pay to go into the pagoda that has many primitive Japanese Buddhist wall paintings.
Address: 1-11-18 Shitennoji, Tennoji-ku, Osaka

Universal Studios Japan
Rather like its American counterpart, Universal Studios Japan is a huge theme park inspired by blockbuster Hollywood movies.
Address: 2-1-33 Sakurajima, Konohana-ku, Osaka

Do

National Bunraku Theater
This is one of the last places in the world where you can still watch bunraku, an intricate form of puppet theater originating from the Edo period. Each of the puppets require three operators. Great Japanese plays of the 1600s and 1700s are accompanied by traditional music and narration. English synopses of the script are provided.
Address: 1-12-10 Nippombashi, Chuo-ku, Osaka

Spa World Complex
The massive Spa World complex in central Osaka is a blend of Japanese baths, Epcot Center, and Las Vegas. In the "European Spa" zone, you'll find themed baths in the styles of Ancient Rome, Greece, Finland, and Atlantis, while in the "Asia Spa" zone, you can bath in Persian and Bali-style pools. There is also a gym, an amusement pool, a stone spa, a salon, a restaurant, and a hotel. You can stay there all day for just ¥2,700!
Address: 3-4-24 Ebisu-higashi, Naniwa-ku, Osaka

Dotonburi Neighborhood

Looking for a fun time and not sure where to go? Just get to Dotonburi, and you'll be all set. The area is named for the Dotonbori Canal, and offers plenty of places to play, eat, drink, shop, and sleep. You wouldn't believe the number of arcades, restaurants, amusement facilities, and people!
Address: Chuo-ku, Osaka

Umeda District
Spending your evening in Umeda is a good bet. You can find every variety of international cuisine here, as well as all the after dinner drinks you can gulp down.

Nightlife in Namba
After Umeda, move to Namba, where Osaka's best clubs (or worst, depending on which you prefer) can be found.. These clubs are open every night of the week, note that they do close around 1am during weekdays. On the weekends, you are free to party all night long!

Shop at

Shinsaibashi
Here is Osaka's most famous shopping district, with a good mix of huge department stores, high-end western designer boutiques, and independent shops, catering to shoppers of every budget! Check out Amerika-mura, often shortened to Amemura, that is espeically popular among young people.

Eat

Once the rice trading hub of the country, today's Osaka is a gourmand's paradise. Try **okonomiyaki** - the omelet pancake with customizeable filling of your choice. You can find it elsewhere, but it won't be as good as Osaka. Other Osaka staples include **kitsune udon**, thick noodle soup blanketed by fried tofu, and **hakozushi**, sushi pressed flat in a bamboo box. On the street, try out **takoyaki**, ball-shaped octopus fritters. The most adventurous food lover can try **tessa**, sashimi made from poisonous globefish. Certified chefs are trained to leave just a bit of poison to numb your lips, but not enough to stop your heart. Go ahead, take a bite!

SAMPLE ITINERARIES

2 DAY ITINERARY IN KYOTO

One day is definitely not enough to do Kyoto justice. But if that's all you have, hit this list and at least you'll still have seen the best of the city, and have plenty of stories to tell. If you have 2 days, build on the schedule for day one with the itinerary for day 2. In two days, you should be able to get a good sense of Kyoto.

Day 1

Head to Higashiyama and visit the stunning Kiyomizu-dera Temple. Take a stroll down to Maruyama Park, and if you are good on time, stop by the peaceful Shoren-in Temple before having lunch at Nishiki Market.

After lunch, head to Fushimi Inari Shrine, and if you are feeling ambitious, also climb the hills. Enjoy dinner in Higashiyama and after dinner, head to the Gion District for Geisha Watching.

Day 2

Follow the 1 Day Itinerary, and on Day 2, head to Arashiyama for the more scenic natural beauty of the city.

Visit the breathtaking Tenryu-ji Temple, which conveniently leads you to the photogenic Arashiyama Bamboo Forest. If you are good on time, visit the Okochi-Sanso Villa before having lunch in central Arashiyama. If you have children or super-monkey fans, substitute or add Iwatayama Monkey Park to your Arashiyama visit.

After lunch, be sure to visit Kinkaku-ji Temple, or, commonly known as the Golden Pavilion. A taxi may be the most convenient means to get there. If your time allows, visit either Daitoku-ji Temple or Ninna-ji Temple, which are not too far from Kinkaku-ji.

Enjoy your dinner in Central Kyoto and head to the Pontocho Area afterwards to experience Kyoto nightlife.

3 Day Itinerary in Kyoto

Follow the Day 1 and Day 2 itinerary above.

Day 3

On the third day, you can either stay in Kyoto or take an easy day trip to Himeji or Uji.

If you decide to stay in Kyoto, head to Nijo Castle to revisit the one-time power center of imperial Edo. Then,head to the nearby Imperial Park. Be sure to make your visit reservations ahead.

Have lunch nearby in Central Kyoto and after lunch, head to northern Higashiyama to walk down the scenic Philosopher's Path. We recommend starting at Ginkaku-ji (Silver Pavilion). Next, visit any or all of the other beautiful temples on this path, including Honen-in Temple and Nanzen-ji Temple.

Enjoy dinner at Higashiyama or Central Kyoto.

Longer Than 3 Days

If you're visiting Kyoto for more than 3 days, we recommend taking a side trip to nearby gems such as Nara or Osaka. Or, better yet, take the train to experience East Asia's most fascinating metropolis – Tokyo.

WHERE TO STAY IN KYOTO

SPECIAL LODGING TYPES

While there are plenty of western hotels with bellboys and room service in Kyoto, we suggest staying at a **ryokan**. These traditional Japanese inns are an one-of-a-kind experience. There are two types of ryokans: a small traditional-style inn, with wooden buildings, long verandahs, and gardens; a more modern high-rise that are more like a luxury hotel with fancy public baths.

Some ryokans hesitate to take non-Japanese guests, especially those who do not speak Japanese, but some venues especially cater to foreigners. A night for one person with two meals start at ¥8,000 and goes up into the stratosphere. ¥50,000 a night per person is not uncommon for some of the posher ones.

Arguably the best ryokans in Japan can be found right here in Kyoto, specifically in Higashiyama. Listed below are the best of the best, famous for their hospitality, attention to detail, and truly authentic experiences.

a Ryokan

RECOMMENDED PLACES TO STAY

Shiraume
Proprietor Tomoko of Shiraume is known for her thoughtful touches, delicious meals, and great stories about the ryokan and the history of Kyoto.
Address: Shirakawa-hotori, Shinbashi-dori, Gionmachi, Higashiyama-ku, Kyoto

Hotel Mume
Hidden behind a red door in the geisha district, Mume offers a great happy hour, excellent services and reservations at local restaurants that you'd never find on your own.
Address: 261 Shinmonzen dori, Umemotocho, Higashiyama-ku

Ohanabo
A great mid-range ryokan, Ohanabo serves a great kaiseki style dinner in your room, and breakfast in a common room. There is also a hot spring, and yukatas for everyone to wear!

Address: 66-2 Shokuyacho, Shimojuzuyamachi Agaru, Akezudori, Shimogyo-ku | Higashihonganji, Kyoto

Salon Haraguchi Tenseian
This tranquil hotel is located in the middle of Maruyama Park. The owners have a couple of bikes on hand for you to borrow, in case you wanted to explore the city that way.
Address: 7-3 Maruyama-cho, higashiyama-ku, Kyoto

Motonago
Unlike many modernized ryokans, Motonago is the real deal. The bathroom is shared, but you can book it for certain hours to have it for yourself.
Address: 511 Washio-cho, Higashiyama-ku | Nene no Michi, Kyoto

Hiiragya
A bit pricier than the rest, but well worth the splurge. Ask for one of the old rooms next to the garden, and you may not want to leave.
Address: 277 Nakahakusancho, Huyacho Anekoji-agaru, Nakagyo-ku, Kyoto

Ryokan Shimizu
Only 10-15 minutes from Kyoto Station, Shimizu is perfectly situated, and comes with impeccable customer service.
Address: 646 Kagiya-cho, Shimogyo-ku, Kyoto

Maifukan
Great service, and you can choose from western and Japanese style rooms at Maifukan.
Address: Minamimonmae Yasakajinja Gion Higashiyama-ku, Kyoto

Arashiyama Benkei
Many rooms of this ryokan in Arashiyama face the lake. It is also only a short walk from the stunning bamboo forest.

Best of Kyoto

Address: 34 Sagatenryuji Susukinobabacho Ukyo-ku, Kyoto

PLANNING YOUR TRIP

BEST TIME TO VISIT KYOTO

Climate

Weather in Kyoto is temperate year-round, so your visit is sure to be pleasant any time of the year. However, the best times to visit are in the fall, October to November, and in the spring, March to May.

Summer is rather hot and humid, while the winter months can get pretty cold. The rainy season runs from mid-June to July, but it won't rain everyday.

Japanese Holidays/Festivals

New Year is the most important holiday in Japan. The country is essentially shut down between December 30 and January 3.

Hanami, or cherry blossom viewing, takes place in March and April. Japanese organize outdoor picnics en masse, and drink quite a bit. The flowers blossom at slightly different times every year depending on the weather, but Japanese TV, and their audience, track their progress obsessively.

Golden Week, the longest holiday lasting from April 27 to May 6, when there are four public holidays within the week. Everyone goes on extended vacation, plane tickets and hotel prices soar as a result to multiples of normal prices. Try to take your vacation before or after Golden Week, to avoid paying extra.

Major Japanese Holidays

January 1 - **New Year's Day** (ganjitsu or gantan)

January 9 (Second Monday of month) - **Coming-of-Age Day** (seijin no hi)

February 11 - **National Foundation Day** (kenkoku kinen no hi)

March 20 - **Spring Equinox Day** (shunbun no hi)

April 29 - **Showa Day** (showa no hi) - first holiday of Golden Week

May 3 - **Constitution Day** (kenpō kinnenbi)

May 4 - **Greenery Day** (midori no hi)

May 5 - **Children's Day** (kodomo no hi) - last holiday of Golden Week

July 16 (third Monday of month) - **Marine Day** (umi no hi)

September 17 (third Monday of month) - **Respect-for-the-Aged Day** (keirō no hi)

September 22 - **Autumnal Equinox Day** (shuubun no hi)

October 8 (second Monday of month) - Sports Day (taiiku no hi)

November 3 - **Culture Day** (bunka no hi 文化の日)

November 23 - **Labor Thanksgiving Day** (kinrō kansha no hi)

December 23 - **The Emperor's Birthday** (tennō tanjōbi)

EXCHANGE RATES

Unit = Yen (¥)

Rates are calculated at the time of this writing. Please check before your departure for the up-to-date exchange rate.

USD: 1 Dollar = 123 Yen
Canadian Dollar: 1 Dollar = 100 Yen
British Pounds: 1 Pound = 192 Yen
Euro: 1 Euro = 138 Yen
Australian Dollar: 1 Dollar = 95 Yen

VISA INFORMATION

Generally, no visa required for visitors (who do not plan to engage in business in Japan). They can obtain landing permission on arrival without a visa. This is usually valid for a stay of up to 90 days. For more information on visas to Japan, visit: Japanese Ministry of Foreign Affairs website- http://www.mofa.go.jp/j_info/visit/visa/

US: eligible for visa-free stay, up to 90 days
Canada: eligible for visa-free stay, up to 90 days
Australia: eligible for visa-free stay, up to 90 days
United Kingdom: eligible for visa-free stay, up to 180 days
Germany: eligible for visa-free stay, up to 180 days
France: eligible for visa-free stay, up to 90 days

Carrying Your Passport with You

Once in Japan, you must carry your passport (or Alien Registration Card or Residence Card, if applicable) with you at all times. If caught in a random check without it (and nightclub raids are not uncommon), you'll be detained until somebody can fetch it for you. Don't panic - first offenders who apologize are usually let off with a warning

TRANSPORTATION

GETTING IN AND GETTING OUT

By Plane

While Kyoto does not have its own airport, you can fly into one of the airports - Kansai International and Itami - serving nearby Osaka. See below for train and driving options between the cities.

From Kansai
If Osaka is your first stop in Japan, you will be landing in Kansai. After landing, you can catch the Japanese Rail (JR) West Haruka Kansai Airport Limited Express Train, which will take you to Kyoto in 77 minutes, with trains leaving every 30 to 60 minutes. With your passport and a copy of your outbound flight from Japan, you can purchase a one-day JR West Kansai Area Pass for ¥2,000, which is reserved for foreigners only and ¥980 cheaper than a regular priced ticket for this train.

Alternatively, you can catch a limousine bus from Kansai to Kyoto Station, which runs twice an hour and stops at major hotels along the way. Tickets cost ¥2,500 (children ¥1,250) one-way, or ¥4,000 for round-trip. Depending on traffic, the ride should take you between 90 to 135 minutes.

From Itami
If you are flying into Osaka from another Japanese city, you will land in Itami. Once landed, take the limousine bus No. 15, which will get you to Kyoto in an hour, and costs ¥1,280. These buses run three times every hour.

For a cheaper option, take the monorail to Hotarugaike, Hankyu Takarazuka Train Line to Juso, and Hankyu Kyoto Train Line to

Kyoto. This sequence of transfers will take you to Shijō Street in Central Kyoto in about an hour.

By Train

You'll most likely take the Shinkansen bullet train from Tokyo, and arrive at JR Kyoto Station. The express "Nozomi" trains cost ¥13,520 one-way, and take approximate 2.15 hours. You can find "open date" tickets - you can board any train as long as it is not full - for ¥700 to ¥1,000 cheaper if you purchase from a travel agency in either city. Note that you will need to register your ticket at the station to reserve your seat.

Alternatively, the slower "Hikari" trains, with a few more stops along the way, get you between the cities for 2.45 hours. If you have purchased the Japan Rail Pass, you can take the Hikari at no additional charges.

There is also the "kodama" train, which is also free with a JR Pass or ¥9,800 for the Puratto Kodama Ticket if purchased at least one day in advance (and gets you a reserved seat and a free drink). This trip makes more stops, takes 3.45 hours. Note that there is only one kodama train per hour, and a few early morning trains are not eligible for the Puratto Ticket.

Between March 1 and April 10, July 20 and September 10, December 10 and January 10, you can take advantage of the Seishun 18 Ticket, which targets college students on break but is available to everyone, you can travel from Tokyo to Kyoto for ¥8,000. However, a group of three costs ¥3,800 per person, and a group of five costs only ¥2,300 per person. The trip takes 8.30 hours.

By Car

To reach Kyoto by car, you can take the Meishin Expressway between Nagoya and Osaka, but be sure to park on the outskirts of the city and use public transit to get around, as parking is practically non-existent.

By Bus

Buses will likely get you to Kyoto for a cheaper fare compared to the pricy high-speed rail options. Buses from Tokyo will generally take the Tomei Expressway or the Chuo Expressway to Nagoya, then the Meishin Expressway to Kyoto. Such a trip takes 7 to 9 hours depending on the exact route. Many companies offer runs between the cities, find major options below.

Willer Express
Willer operates a number of daytime and overnight buses between Tokyo and Kyoto. An overnight one-way ticket starts around ¥3,800 for standard seating, up to ¥9,800 in luxury shell seating. You can book tickets on their English website (http://willerexpress.com/en/), or purchase a Willer's Japan Bus Pass if you are traveling to other cities in Japan.

JR Bus
Another major bus operator on the Tokyo-Kyoto route, JR Bus does not take online reservations in English, but you can visit a train station to reserve seats. The company offers 2x2 Seishun youth buses, 1x1x1 standard buses with individual seats, and premium buses with wider seats and more amenities. Expect to pay around ¥3,500 for an overnight trip on a Seishun bus, ¥7,600 for the premium bus. Daytime fares start from ¥5,000. Tickets run higher on weekends and holidays.

Hankyu Bus
Overnight fares start from ¥7,950.

Keihan Bus

Discount bus fares start around ¥5,000. Regular bus fares start around ¥8,180.

Kintetsu Bus
"Flying Sneaker" discount bus fares start from ¥3,900 with advance purchase. Regular "Flying Liner" bus fares start from ¥6,320.

GETTING AROUND

By Public Transport

Like other major Japanese cities, Kyoto has a well-developed and highly efficient public transit system. For planning purposes, check out HyperDia (http://www.hyperdia.com/en/) which references both public and private trains, buses, and subway lines.

Train
Kyoto has several train lines, all helpfully sign-posted in English. The Keihan train line is useful for eastern Kyoto, the two Keifuku tram lines are helpful for northwestern Kyoto. The Hankyu line can be used to reach Arashiyama, and runs all the way to Osaka and Kobe. JR lines run from Kyoto Station to the northwestern, southwestern, and southeastern regions.

Subway
There are only two subway lines in Kyoto, serving a small part of the city. The Karasuma line runs north-south under Kyoto Station, while the Tozai line runs west-east. Both lines are useful for traveling in city center, but do not reach the many temples you will want to see.

A one-day pass for the subway costs ¥ 600.

Bus

This is the best and only practical public transportation option for tourists. Confusingly, there are two bus companies, but you will most likely be taking the green and white Kyoto City Buses, which serves the city, while the red and white Kyoto Buses serving the suburbs will be minimally useful to you.

Make note of the Raku Bus, which has three routes (100, 101, and 102). These skip many non-tourist stops, and are a great way to hit the tourist spots quickly.

Bus fares are fixed at ¥220, but for a day of sightseeing, consider purchase a one-day pass, which costs ¥500 for adults and ¥250 for children under 12. You can buy day passes directly from the bus driver, or from the bus information center just outside Kyoto Station, the major hub of all bus lines. You can also buy a combined unlimited subway and bus 1-day pass for ¥1,200, or a combined 2-day pass for ¥2,000.

While you are buying a pass at the information center, be sure to ask for a "Bus Navi" leaflet, which contains a route map for the bus lines to most sights.

By Bicycle

When in Kyoto, ride as the locals ride. Consider renting a bike to get around the city. On bike, you can cut through back alleys that are quieter, and avoid being stuck in traffic with all the buses during the height of the tourist season.

There are bike rentals all over the city. Just remember, you need to ride and drive on the left-hand side of the road in Japan!

ESSENTIAL JAPANESE CULTURE TO KNOW

Tipping

Tips are not expected in Japan, even though the country's service is legendary. Attempting to tip from a westerner can even be seen as an insult, and the wait staff is likely to run after you to return the money you "forgot". Unless you are in a high-end ryokan or with an English-speaking tour guide, you are safer not to tip.

Manners and Showing Respect

As with many East Asian cultures, a person's family name comes before their given name in Japan. In addition, using only someone's given name when speaking to or about them is very personal, and should only be used between close friends. At all other times, use family name plus -san, a suffix approximately like "Mr." or "Ms."

Japanese people bow to greet each other, even when they are on the phone! As a foreigner, try to at least bob your head to greet your Japanese associates. Sometimes, in order to be accommodating, Japanese will offer a handshake to a westerner.

Be on time! There is no such thing as "fashionably late" in Japan. You will only be considered rude.

There is no strict dress code when visiting temples and shrines, but you will feel out of place in shorts or other revealing clothes. Jeans and casual clothing are fine, but remember to remove your shoes when entering temples. There are usually slippers for you to change into.

Japan has an avid drinking culture. Never refuse a drink - it's considered very rude - but accept it and sip at your drink. Make sure your glass is half full.

USEFUL JAPANESE TERMS AND PHRASES

You'll likely be able to find someone who speaks English and is willing to help you in Japan, famous for their hospitality, but it's always good to have a few key phrases at your command, and to show your politeness and respect with new friends you might make. Remember, to be safe, address everyone by their last name, with -san attached.

Thank you: Arigatoo gozaimasu.

Thank you very much: Doomo arigatoo gozaimasu.

You're welcome: Doo itashimashite.

Please: onegai shimasu

Yes: hai

No: iie

Excuse me: Sumimasen.

Pardon me: Sumimasen.

I'm sorry: Gomen'nasai.

I don't understand: Wakarimasen.

I don't speak Japanese: Nihongo ga wakarimasen.

I don't speak Japanese very well: Nihongo wa amari joozu ja arimasen.

Do you speak English: Eigo o hanashimasu ka?

Speak slowly, please: Yukkuri hanashite kudasai.

Repeat, please: Moo ichido onegai shimasu.

What's your name: Onamae wa nandesu ka?

How are you: Ogenki desu ka?

Do you speak English: Eigo o hanashimasu ka?

Where is the subway: Chikatetsu wa doko desu ka?

Is the tip included: Chippu wa fukumarete imasu ka?

How much does that cost: Kore wa ikura desu ka?

Is there a public phone here: Koko ni kooshuudenwa ga arimasu ka?

Can I get on the internet: Intaanetto o tsukattemo iidesu ka?

Can you help me: Tetsudatte itadakemasu ka?

Where is the bathroom: Ofuro wa doko desu ka?

-dori: Street/Avenue

REFERENCE INFORMATION

Ministry of Foreign Affairs of Japan - Visa Information
http://www.mofa.go.jp/j_info/visit/visa/

Kyoto Prefecture Website
http://www.pref.kyoto.jp/visitkyoto/en/

East Japan Railway Company (JR)
http://www.jreast.co.jp/e/

For Public Transportation Planning
http://www.hyperdia.com/en/

Application for Visiting The Imperial Palace, Sento Imperial Palace, Katsura Imperial Villa, and Shugakuin Imperial Villa
http://sankan.kunaicho.go.jp/english/

CONCLUSION

We hope this pocket guide helps you navigate Kyoto and find the most memorable and authentic things to do, see, and eat.

Thank you for purchasing our pocket guide. After you've read this guide, we'd really appreciate your honest book review!

Sincerely,
The Wanderlust Pocket Guides Team

CREDITS

Cover photo source: Flickr
Map of Kyoto and Map of Japan original vector source: Wikipedia commons

COPYRIGHT AND DISCLAIMER

45534193R00046

Made in the USA
Lexington, KY
30 September 2015